Thieves in the Afterlife

Kendra DeColo

saturnalia books

Distributed by University Press of New England
Hanover and London

Saturnalia Books
105 Woodside Rd.
Ardmore, PA 19003
info@saturnaliabooks.com

ISBN: 978-0-9899797-0-2
Library of Congress Control Number: 2013951637

Book Design by Saturnalia Books
Printing by Westcan Printing Group, Canada

Cover Art: Harmony Korine

Cover Design: Michael Carney

Author Photo: Lindsey Rome

Distributed by:
University Press of New England
1 Court Street
Lebanon, NH 03766
800-421-1561

Sincere gratitude to the editors of the following publications where these poems first appeared, at times in earlier versions:

Borderlands- Texas Poetry Review: "Through a Small Town"

Calyx: "The Healing" and "God is a Capitalist"

Native: "Ode In Which I Pee Standing Up"

Muzzle: "Avocados" and "After Hours, Provincetown Cemetery"

Printer's Devil Review: "The Dream in Which You Are"

Southern Indiana Review: "Confession with Fire"

Split This Rock: Poems of Witness and Provocation: "The Strap-On Speaks"

Tupelo Quarterly: "Rodney Dangerfield's Ex" and "Vajazzled"

The Collagist: "Anthem," "Blue and Green Music," and "The Vocalist"

Vinyl Poetry: "Barnacle" and "The Guitarist"

"The Dream in Which You Are" appears in *Best Indie Lit New England*, edited by Thomas A. Dodson.

"After Hours Anthem" appears in *EDNA: A Journal of the Millay Colony for the Arts*.

"After the Poet from Kentucky...," "Avocados," "God is a Capitalist," and "Places Where I Would Like to Conceive" all appear in *Poetry Sucks! An Anthology of Poetry, Music, and All Sorts of Bad Language*, edited by Chet Weise and Ben Swank (Third Man Books, 2014).

Thank you Yusef Komunyakaa for choosing the book. Thank you to Henry Israeli and Sarah Blake for your vision and support.

Endless thanks to the Tennessee Arts Commission, the Millay Colony for the Arts, the Bread Loaf Writer's Conference, Split This Rock Poetry Festival, and Vanderbilt's MFA Program where many of these poems came into being.

Thank you to the following people whose friendship, inspiration, and generosity helped make this book possible: Rosa Aleman, Dorothy Antczak, Richard and Lydia Ayoade, Beth Bachmann, Haywood Berman, Melissa Cundieff-Pexa, the Einhorn family, Katie Greene, Rex Hussman, T.J. Jarrett, Harmony Korine, Susanna Kwan, Tal Beery and Eugenia Manwelyan, Alice Neiley, Ayesha Nur, Mahra Parian, Tracey Primavera, Stephanie Pruitt, Margaret Roark, Liz Santiago, Molly Siegel, Christina Stoddard, and Phillip B. Williams.

Thank you to the teachers who have been lights along the way: Kate Daniels, Nikky Finney, Ross Gay, Peter Goddard, Peter Guralnick, Terrance Hayes, Rick Hilles, Major Jackson, and Mark Jarman.

Special and most heartfelt thanks to Jeffrey McDaniel, teacher, mentor, and friend.

Thank you Tyler Mills, Matthew Olzmann, Katherine Sullivan, Bridget Talone, and Elizabeth Townsend for your encouragement and belief in the manuscript.

Thank you Jennifer and Keith Leonard, Tyler Mills, Matthew Olzmann, Katherine Sullivan, Bridget Talone, and Elizabeth Townsend for your encouragement and belief in the manuscript.

To my family, for everything. This book is for you.

And for Avi, my home. We took it by force.

for my family

Table of Contents

Yes, I have a pretty good idea what beauty is. It survives alright. It aches like an open book. It makes it difficult to live.

—Terrance Hayes

I. GUSH AND EPHEMERA

Anthem

"I Heart Pussy"

Whoever believed these words
       enough to carve each letter
              into the green paint

of a bench drizzled with leaves
       one autumn, must have loved, too, the heat
              of the word

as it flushed from heart to finger,
       slipped through the throat like a koi
              in a corporate pond

how you can say it sober
       on a clear morning
              and let the murk sprawl

open the inner eye, mouth
       stunned with the church-musk
              of syllables

each cut and stroke
       made holy with gush
              and ephemera.

He or she must have felt the word
       pierce the core of their lopsided
              heart until it gleamed

in the gouged wood, must have
        stood on the bench like the president
           of all the strip malls

of America, dressed in smoke
        and aftershave, wanting to shout:
           Praise the under-shimmer

and bisected vowel! The world
        belongs to the panty-less
           and unshaved.

God bless the subwoofer and carnival
        ride-hitching, the jukebox
           junkies, five-and-dime

store thieving laureate
        of all things counterfeit
           and candescent.

He or she must have
        believed in a world where Pussy
           is king, where all day Pussy

rides the subways of the heart
        illuminating the anthems
           scrawled there,

what is too precious
        to be said aloud,
           what is so beautiful it's a sin.

Avocados

Let's get wasted as avocados,
      solemn and shapely
            in their alligator skins, lucid, sweet-talking

lovers laid bare on rough blankets,
      two-for-a-dollar magic
         sacked and clutched

in a child's alleyway
      hand. Let's get foamed, salty-eyed,
         dismembered into smoothness,

gilded and glyphed
      onto a retired stripper's back, smoked
        and spooled, shucked

to a mineral glow. Let's get stupid. Opalescent.
      God-complexioned. Viscera strangled
        to a shimmer. Ghosted, vanquished,

sticky as hashish, lacquered and whispered
      into the Guadalquivir's ear. Let's get squalid and romantic
      in the squid-pink light

roughing up the tulips, then let's stumble
      down the throat of 3 a.m.
        to the titty bar

where Magda will stroke our faces
      before breaking our jaws
        with those ungodly breasts

and we will cry out with a tenderness
      that betrays our hunger, our voices
          thatched into a roof

that collapses under her weight,
      twinkle like half-formed
          hearts terrorizing

her vastness, green and wild as
      another country. Bearable
          music wincing between moans.

After Hours, Provincetown Cemetery

Tonight my dead are restless,
    reinventing themselves
        with names like *Glissando*

and *Surreptitious*. I want a tree
    to be a tree again, not this trick
        of light, chaos of muscle curved

into the neck of a violin.
    Autumn welds itself
        to the seams of August

and we are saddled by its heat,
    the heart of silence
        smooth as a gun.

You are somewhere
    iridescent and unholy,
        sharp horizon of a man,

traveling circus broken
    into luminous machinery,
        caravan pounding like horses

along the highway. You,
    dog-toothed piano,
        Queen whose glittered

lashes eat up the dark.
    Your words are thumbprints
        on the eyelids of the gods.

Your body is the book
    I break into, hijacked
        of meaning. Your voice,

ejaculation of moonlight,
    your speeding ticket sex, gold-veined
        heart—tonight you are

my only shelter. I inhabit you
    like a squatter, burning my one small light
        in this cemetery of thieves.

Barnacle

Barnacle, I would like to be remade in your image,
hollowed tooth, dress of calcium, blue-salt tongue. Your language
of echoes colonizes the Earth's cold thighs. I want it ·
as I sometimes want the uncomplicated diminuendo of my life,
to disperse and fade, blurred into the music of bees, thirst, words
scratched into plexiglass, this being human such a dirty business.
I crave your sterile logic, philosopher's beard glittering with fleas.
Clutter of fossils, oxidized starlight, fist of loaded dice, three-
card hustler of the sea—You, rapture of knuckles along the mouth.
You suicide letter of glee, treble clef kiss, alphabet
of orgasms and mineral lung. You bootlegger of miracles, preacher
with a lisp. You stripper's robe on the dressing room floor,
slow cooker of meth, glint of gold in the blues singer's mouth.
You rickshaw vanity plate, you ten-part harmony of sweat
grinding on a corner—Your solemn voice proliferates like spores,
your junky arm bloated with jewels, your face of scars made of history
and indifference—You breeder of ghosts, you sprawl of eyes,
you flock of unborn children haunting my small city.

Clitoris

More alarm clock than emergency
lever. More Muzak than jazz. Between fields

of iridescence and a kingdom jaundiced
with heaven you choose to live

incognito. Your rap sheet is decent
as a prisoner earning good time

in the library, eating pages of the dictionary
to stay alive. What rocks have you pocketed,

wanting to be more mineral than flesh, opal
tongued, inefficient machine invented

to stave off loneliness? Why won't you
admit you're selfish, that you'd rather

live lit by your own flame and burn
out than sustain a collective glow?

You're as interesting as the cracked
molar wincing every time whiskey

passes my jaw. You live in a strip
mall where old people overdose

on pheromones. When chain-smoking
girls flick their cherries, you seethe

with envy, to be that shade of power,
narcotic and smoldering a croon.

Naples

City of bladed mornings and hard women,
bazaar of hustlers pawning sheet music, baby teeth, arms
of octopus pocked and stinging,

it's hard to believe you are not mine.
Even your ghosts wear my face,
calling me into arenas of dirt

where bulls fall to their knees
diaphanous with sorrow, gleaning music
from dregs of fountains.

But Naples, you touch me
with the unshaved lips of an urchin,
thick clouds of smog roiling

from motors, roots of fig trees
spiraling up like tongues. Your ego
is equal to nothing but itself,

your skin sequined with salt
like a topography of wishes.
Where hands once breathed desire

to make something out of this ancient
circus, the streak of my purple dress
lights a ruin, blood thick

with the hustle and hum
of every man who said they'd never
leave. I see you as I see myself

through their eyes, oracular
as a love song played on a half-strung guitar
while the ship sails away.

Places Where I Would Like to Conceive

The cathedral outside Memphis
whose voluptuous seams
hold in a riot of prayer,
strung-out saints
washing away dusk's
graffiti. The steps
of the Imperial War
Museum, its arsenal
of leaves and rain,
thighs embroidered
with perpetual winter, glass
tanks of bullets, anemic
handwriting of soldiers'
letters home. I would like
to conceive inside money
factories. Exhibits
of expired maps. The glacier
I loved for its green arms
and misshapen mouth.
Django's pockets
of static. Stadiums
where silence bleeds
into history. I would like
to conceive atop
the world's tallest
elevator. I would like to

conceive holding hands
with your ghost
after drinking too much
and cavorting
with the stray dogs
of Cerro Alegre,
riding up and down
alleys of the city we love,
whose children bear the gleam
of your ruinous face.

When You Dance Remember the Half-Finished World

of low tide, the bleached
hieroglyphics of fossils

siphoning murk from salty
hearts. I'm half in love

with the rowboat turned
on its side, limp scuffle

of crab whose bottled tongues
distill the night in long drags, a vapor

I want to embody like my mother
snapping off her gloves

for a cigarette before returning
to the conveyor belt's

iridescence, the blurred resonance
of blade against sieved

shadow and bone. I want to praise
the intricacies of her wrist,

its breath and light, the machine
whose starry teeth I will never

touch and yet pulls my existence
into its hemming, my body precise

as it is monotonous, living
beyond what joy I can afford

and asking for nothing but a stain
equal in hue to the force

of my living, to remember
my first language is darkness,

gesture, the light devoured
between two bodies,

hands dissolved,
mending what can't be seen.

II. THE MAN IN ME

Gary Coleman's Face

First, let me admit that I'm a failure
which is to say
      this avuncular battle cry and balls-out

salute, this swollen image
disproportioned across your left ass cheek
      speaks to me as it stares back

at the camera, expression of stunned
rapture mixed with surrender
as if the artist who wrestled Coleman's face

onto your pastry-colored skin, held his neck
while you sang your favorite drunken
anthem and buddies cheered you on,

believed a higher power lurked inside
the ink. Once, driving my sister home
      from the police station where she'd

spent the night for public indecency
      we passed a body as it disappeared
into a zippered bag, glimpsed the hand

starred in an ashy fist. The next day
she carved CUNT onto the inside
of her lower lip, scrawled and crow-tongued

as a man's shut lids. I never watched
Diff'rent Strokes or understood
how a man must carry the weight

of his oversized heart, but if there's foolishness
        in any attempt to get things right
let me admire this gesture, too, as a failure

to admit what I am: scouring
for signs of hope in the self-
destructive acts of others, moved by anyone

willing to let themselves be branded
by what they love, irreparably,
perfectly damaged.

Rodney Dangerfield's Ex Writes Him a Letter

"I tell ya, my wife likes to talk during sex. Last night she called me from a motel."
—Rodney Dangerfield

How I fell in love with you: your eyes
wild as the moon, pocked and studded

with heaven. I liked to suck
smoke from your mouth. It tasted

sharp as a field of onions. Spaetzle.
The inside of a boot. I was happy

to be the bad cook, slut, fat lady
giving directions to her body

as if I were notes spilled through
a giant horn, conjured from your lips

like a dark feast. I remember
how your voice swung disembodied

as shoes from a telephone wire
when I called to tell you I'd just

made love at the drive-in. We watched
Easy Money and wrecked the insides

of one another, tussling in the sweaty
weather of your image, his fist

a star breaking inside my liver.
I became a telephone booth, open

as an observatory for watching
galaxies huff like horses. Your voice

was lost and everywhere.
Most of all I knew I did not

want my body back. I tell you
and already hear it aching

inside a joke. Don't think I ever
wanted more than this.

The Barber Shop

I loved to watch the precision
of razor against another's scalp,

glossy seams released like horizons

dividing water and sky, what I believed
most men could never do—

sending daughters to school unbrushed,

split ends strangled into rubber bands.
Here, tenderness is a tether,

head pulled towards the chest,

warmed by the barber's palms,
his focus split between work

and the hum of telenovelas, metal

tables stacked and gleaming
with cards, a line of men,

loose and unbraided,

waiting for fingers, as if touch
could make one whole

day become a year, skin kissed

where hair is shaved away, touch
enough to make you need the one

who holds the razor in his hand.

Ode to the One-Liner

Remember the way Rodney could move
through a crowded room

fluid as a dancer, ready
to pull a punchline

from overheard slang, tug
the dreamy entrails

of non sequitur into a joke? Maybe
the saddest thing

isn't a fat man
drenched in hard light

sweating for a faceless
crowd. In the dark he turns

to his wife one last time
and asks her to pull

his heart inside-out
like a sleeve. He says:

I would like to mint
a coin from the smooth

ditch of your ear, and
the first time we made love

I wanted to turn off
the lights so I could

see you better.
If I'm a fool, let it mean

I made things for you
out of nothing. Let it be

my pockets were bright
doves waiting.

After the Poet From Kentucky Tells Me My Poems Are Not Considerate to Their Audience I Try to Teach Him What I Know About Etiquette

When a lover waits for me to come,
I say thank you. When a lover
comes in my mouth,
I say you're welcome.
He runs his hand across
the pages like a priest,
breath full of bourbon
aftermath, crooked rows
of teeth like pews
in a musty tabernacle.
He jams his thumb again
at the misplaced simile
as if to say
straighten out darlin,
join the right side
and get a Camry.
Something about misogyny
makes my clit grow
seven throbbing inches.

Sex Shop for Transcendentalists

All genderlessness is not made equal
by throwing oneself, say, into a traffic of electric hummingbirds.
Consider the clairvoyant's cellar of paraphernalia:
dildos thick as telescopes in every shade of skin,
effervescent lips of viscera like an entrance to another world,
finding yourself in a bedroom strewn with fisticuffs, fast food wrappers,
God lounging in his skivvies.
Hot and gritty as a windshield in July,
isn't it a miracle to think how many men each night
jack off to the same image?
Kind of like synchronicity for pervs
like when I woke in a bus station bathroom,
my forehead annotated with premonitions—
Nostradamus type scripture stitched at the brow.
O is the sound our patron saint makes
plucking initials from inky limbs,
quilted litanies of epidemics, stilted
requiems, catalogs of
STDs for every season beginning alphabetically.
Take it by force, she whispers through the hum of machines,
undulating her tongue in every dialect of blue:
venal, vagrant, vaporish,
wet as the wild bucking mist, the dream where
Xena presses her machete to my throat.
Yes, I chose pleasure over redemption. Call it
Zen cashed in for desire.

Vajazzled

Reef-ridged and polyglottal,
spangled concussion lisped

and asphyxiating
in a room of radiators

who asked you to be discreet?
Plush hieroglyphics, aurora-

tinctured atmosphere. When
flush with sequins you're

incognito as bad air,
loose notes swarming

a honeyed asylum.
Watching you grin

on TV selling bruised
syntax to prepubescent

girls, the twitch
of electricity savored

on lips, *Bitch*
sounds almost beautiful

as in, make me
your bitch.

Carnivore in drag,
inextinguishable flare—

don't stop
until each eye

fans open in us
like a prayer.

The Dream in Which You Are

Inside of me—
half-human, half collected
fragments of morning walks
along the wintered cathedrals
and brown stones
of Mass Ave.—

you've seen my body
            so many times
you can recall perfectly
the deep cracks of my
white-bottomed feet,
the air odored as I taste:

gin and earnings of week-
long sweat. My skin
stiff in your mouth—
I'm inside of you as much
as you're inside of me—

working against anonymous
parts, newsprint crackling
within the flint of my slacks

as you raise my legs
to go deeper, noticing
my face blurred

below the neon orange
wool of my cap,
a numb light streaking
over us inside the ATM

and you can't tell
whether I'm human
or not, what sex
inside the heap
of bulged plastic, the blunt
truth of my tongue

reaching towards you, my stench,
wadded and wet, all of me
one held breath,
waiting to pass a needle
through this difficult sleep.
When you wake, part of me

will still be there
faceless and shadow-
skinned, my genitals
x-ed out, signed
over the length
of your long,
immaculate life.

The Strap-On Speaks

It is easy to believe
we are separate entities,

you and I

as I wait, a fish in the chasm
of a drawer
                inhabiting the silk
        and dust scored dark,

biding my time
                until the need arises,

I, who was created
not to bear witness,

bleed, speak,

but make you more fully
                who you are,

        filling space
as a bloomed,
                hardened thing,

unarticulated flesh,
                demanding

dreams through pressed lids
and glands, lips
                swallowing

some blue throb
        of magic.

　　~

At times, we blur
and I don't know which of us
        this harness means
                        to possess,

strapped with wings,
        the shorn heaven

'of back and ass
        dividing shadows,
rising from
        the burning fields among us.

　　~

I want to be your tongue
        torching a city,

a storm wrenched
        into formlessness

as the threat of a wave.

　　~

What am I to you
if not the climb
        towards blinding light,

unmappable intimacies,
if not this apathy
                    of reckless stars

where you buck,
            dizzy with atmosphere,

the compass of me swiveling
at the root.

What am I
if not vein, vessel,

if not phantom
            spinning inside flesh,
no lust to speak of,

and what of me
            remains, I wonder,

in your hollows,
            ghosted muscle
cusping your instep,

a soreness of aura,
blistered air.

If we ever get to where
            we want to go,

I swear I will erupt
       as a wingless bird,

carried up by my own
       bloodless imagination,

untethered
       as the hand of a god.

Ode in Which I Pee Standing Up

Like a drunk staggering home
through a field
of slit-open blossoms

lit up and green as a jukebox
or the man leaning behind the club
astonished by his own

heat and immense
echo threading the moon-
slathered alley

I pee standing up too
in love with the v
my legs make straddling
a shadow

the phosphorus hiss
of night air
fingers slicing mist

in love with the teeth
of my hand as it smiles

the pulled curtain of rain
and wooziness

curled tongues
of lamps

Because the walk home
is full of too many
bridges whose slang

the river can't understand
sleek and innocuous
always having to look
up at the same rootless dark

Because the stars
are impotent
but I am not

the field accosted
by wings
scuffled and flame-throated
with eyes like ghosts

I know how
to work flesh into useful
contortions

blossoms or boats

the way a body
bends to hijack the shape
of another's breath

each note of praise
lodged in the octaves'
cold arc

Because to pray is to listen
each cell hustling in my liver
letting the hands

of light shake me down

III. THIEVES IN THE AFTERLIFE

Through a Small Town

"The truck was incinerated, and it is still burning."
                                    —*NY Times, July 3, 2010*

They heard music
before they heard the storm

before the truck piled
onto the side of road

that ran dusty and snake-skinned
through a small town

a flock swelling
inside the ribs of thin trees

and where the road spiked
a finger towards the river

where the river
was the voice of a woman

walking backwards
into a dream

where they dreamed
of running the sky

where the sky swallowed
birds and music and where

children had taught themselves
to gather air and gasoline

and a dog now makes circles
in the ash and damp

dirt spits up an oily heart
and where red birds pierce the dusk

a woman stabs
her shovel into the ground

works through sweat
and insects eating her arms

until she stands in the deep
not knowing how or what

where the road was a ripped
vein and the night bled oil

and bodies swallowed up
in the green music

and if you have ever followed
singing down a dark path

arriving at a church hushed
with the enormous eyes

of the living like wet leaves
turning through you

tell me who you thank
when you step out into the world

where a tree has wasted
its blossoms at your feet.

My Attempt to Write Honestly About Race

Don't worry, no one wants that flat ass
Haywood shouts through the cracked-open window

at the blonde who clutches something invisible
to her chest. *Fucking honkies* I used to say

in college whenever we'd pass frat row, the astro-
turf lawns festooned with plastic cups. The streetlamps

flicker like auras, illuminating the teeth
of run-down porches. The girl's hair flashes

behind us like a siren. *White bitch* stings worse
than bitch. We drive all night until the moon pounds

like a hangover in the rearview. Like the eyes of children
who followed me in another country, made tiny guns

with their hands. I weave my fingers through the cold
air, listening to Haywood's laughter until waves

of music convulse over us and I'm saved
again from seeing what I am.

After Hours, Boston

Play memories of silk
scratched in the palm.
Play strap against a mouth
of milk and moonshine.
It's not enough to save a body
from darkness but teach one to shine.
Play Sequined Hips.
Drinkable Midnight. Play
Bach's Blues. Troubled
Tongue. Razor-burned
Woman. Play the hard edge
of a century stacked
with ruin

the way you fake your death
each night
composing perfect
elegies, selling hymns
to hardened faces,
how you play god
to a godless room.

The Guitarist

Wes Montgomery & James Clay, Hollywood 1958

It's the look of terror on his face,
the glossy flank of an open grand piano
untouched & muscled with light
behind them, that makes me turn
away, the saxophonist leaning
into the curve of breath, the arc
glinting from his lips, almost
unwieldy, thick-limbed, the precision
of a volt striking the ground. He is cruel,
I think, lips gripping the brass
mouth & wood tongue, because
he knows he can't be touched
as the fighter who doubles
inside the ring, winged fits
of blood & electricity, humming
like a halo around the near-corpse
of the man he's whipped, fists
demarcating notes into the haze
between them, the guitarist's mouth
& eyes swollen with knowledge
he is ill-equipped, his left hand
a culled constellation, flaccid above
the strings as if to form the chord
of a blistering universe, the first
cut into darkness, deliberate chaos
of the child who pretends to play,
lifting the wooden body to his chest,

who knows what stirs in his cells
has no name, the crook & jag, blue
smoke, a bud opening in his abdomen,
swelled to the size of hope, as we become
the shape of whatever we hold
in our hands when asked to lift up
what we cannot bear to touch.

The Year I Worked in a Prison

I was a woman naked inside an invisible
uniform. I thought I had flesh to spare,

that I could put my soul out on the sidewalk,
crush it under my heel and resurrect
its jaws of smoke around a streetlamp.

I didn't know skin could absorb the hiss
of a man drowning in his own desire,

that walls mimic two bodies grinding
into one another, whose urgent music
sped the hours needled into the bloodstream.

The day I found my car shot
I wasn't thinking about god.

The dirt was frozen and buried under snow.
A woman stood next to me trying hard to communicate
with a fist flickering in a window. Not god

or my hands, gloveless and burning
through stacks of time.

When It Rained

                    that summer outside unit 1-2-1
        it scattered like a sack of rice
                                            a rinse of beetle skins

        collecting in a bucket below the leak we bowed through
                                            like a holy entrance into
        the classroom

        where it was too hot or too cold & the men leaned over

                their notebooks until lightning sliced

                                    the skylight   one long arm
        hammered into the glass

                                someone poured kool-aid into the rainwater
        frothy-red
                as spat-up blood

                        that summer

                my second   his fourth since he was eighteen & getting out
        soon
                it would be August & humid

                                he knew he wouldn't last a week

                called us crying when he lost his mother's number
        showed up in the lobby

sweat pouring from his hands

                         into mine

                    I tried to bike home over the Charles

the smell of his skin
honeycombed in the river

          deeper into the swish

that hardened to hail until I couldn't see the road
       & turned back

          humming through what stung like heaven

After Hours Anthem

Let's return to aisles of mollusks and fire
escapes, this world where bodies gleam

in fresh supplies of moonlight and a DJ
hems pulse to echo. Let's return to fields

of discarded knives. Infinite aquariums
and fingernail files. Let's re-enter and loot

the sheen from every shade of blue,
the curl of dissonance from tongued

anthems. You say you only have room
for sadness, smuggled over the border

for when you need to feel human again,
to remember the kiss of smoke and gin,

cursive of rain between a woman's legs.
What does misuse and superfluous mean

in this over-stocked world? The get-away
car is revved, my dress camouflaged

with streetlamps and crows. Won't you
take sips with me from this spill

of bootlegged heaven, say fuck it
to eternal sleep and fill our pockets

with the canteen of every song,
every mouth burning in the choir?

Won't you stand with me, guiltless,
and praise all we're still waiting to become?

After Seeing *The Misfits*

I want to taste the grit
in Marilyn's throat, her breath, shattered
and sapphire, guarding the edges of things. I want the hive
of panic in her lungs, the rim of a hoof planted in the Earth's
skull, to pull at the root of a feeling and see its shimmered tip
spasm with grief. There are rooms
in my heart I still cannot enter. One
belongs to my sister, wearing teeth around her neck
and selling glimpses of a carved universe, her veins
pierced with phosphorescence.
Listening to the bodies of horses tremble in the half-dark
I want to remember the smell of her hair,
its blue star radiating my chest. To reach through
the scrim of milky light
and touch the injured mare who cradles us in her muzzle.
To believe in a god so obscene
she cannot stop loving us
is to believe in our own goodness, no matter
how rough and unearthed, that one day I will love
back with the indigence of my body. Will hear the roar begin
in my palms and catch fire.

Something to Vaporize Inside of

By the end of summer my tongue
was the size of a flask in a hitchhiker's pocket,
a swiveling road making small talk with dust
particles. I kept wanting more and more of it:
the temple-shaped clouds crowding
the skyline, a bad movie glittering against
the bus window, hung like a chandelier
inside the pulp of infinite rooms.
It smelled of oranges and I made up
for lost time, inventing flavors for each
shade of blue tucked into the leaves
of passing trees. The rain came, slashing
the clouds until they oozed into one another
like silver, like flesh swallowing
a bullet and squeezing out a seed. The way a star
can rip open the night sky and you can't tell
how many seconds it took, stunned
in the after-light, wanting to hoard each kernel,
each fissure, each spark inside the world's
tallest elevator, shanty towns built of scrap-
light for people like us who know angels
do the dirty work, collecting the beauty
we waste: this achy vein of road and air,
insatiable cloud shaped like the fire's
imagination, coming home if only to let
my heart flash its gills, erupt into an epilepsy

of minnow at your feet, for the things
we loved, against, inside of, for the things
we won't survive, the taste of summer
and all that will be there without us,
materializing in the sweet vapor.

What I Loved

Suffolk County House of Corrections

In the beginning there were the hands
of a clock doing obscene things with time,
the soundlessness of cells locked
with one enormous wand. There were nails
to be chewed and papers to correct.
There were aluminum tables smeared
with breakfast grease.

There was a mouse someone kept
as a pet until it escaped and was pounded
to death with a sneaker. There was beige,
then yellow, then bloodshot. There was the bullet
hole in the back of the neck that made him
walk with a cane, tilt his head over
a tiny bible. There was the circle of men
passing the invisible microphone.

There was canteen spread in the mornings,
plastic bags of tuna, toothpaste, pens, jolly ranchers,
the waiting in a metal doorframe.
There was the smell of chili and cheese
microwaved in plastic bowls, the Chef
who could make anything from *lo mein*
to *pasta e fagioli* and the student's mouth
around a green apple.

There were morning erections
and untrimmed fingernails,
fists pounding out a message,
girlfriends outside squinting up to see.
There were love poems signed
your friend and *respectfully.*
There were little sisters shot
in front of ice cream stores.
There were daughters burned
alive on the third floor of an apartment
found in the closet welded
into each others' arms.

There was the puddle of sun
across a freshly waxed floor.
There was *The Prophet* worn
to feathers in his golden hands.
There was Coltrane and Slow Jams.
There was *hello* and *good-bye,*
get home safe, have a nice ride
and *why do you smile*
all the time? There was leaving
and feeling like I never left,
the boy raped in another unit
and taken to the hospital.
There was the black German Shepherd
biting at the leash, the pissing
into a towel in the middle of the night,
and the Hole, deeper and darker

than the shrine pit of imagination,
hard enough to grind your threshold
into a thousand headlights.

There was the restraining order
that sent him back, away from the woman
he loved and wrote to everyday,
and the letter that never came.
There was the jar of fireflies
he caught with his sister
in the backyard that didn't exist,
the rubble of his inner arm,
the tattoo across an abdomen
that said *sucker free,*
the blood's infected museum,
the voice that swelled like Paul Robeson,
muting the linoleum in velvet
inside the empty classroom.
There was the church, the coffin,
the hush, the mosque, the block,
the ache, the last time, the hope,
the lesson I searched for in each cell
of my heart, was the heart I offered up,
placed into the dark, onto the sawdust,
was the inside-out womb, the wasting
away, was the world waiting
with a purpose, gleaming
across the stage like a diploma,
wind dividing bodies in flight.

IV. GOD IS A CAPITALIST

Blue and Green Music

after the painting by Georgia O'Keeffe

Tonight I'm in the crowd
        aching to enclose the woman
                who strips off petals

of stolen light, to touch the rim
        of static before nakedness
                is another closing

door. If pleasure cannot be asked
        but given into, why do I come here
                if only to be unseen?

When we lived together
        my sister returned
                each night laced

in dregs of glitter
        to study after long shifts
                of letting customers buy her

drinks, never telling them
        her real name. Now I understand
                what keeps us whole

is the face of daylight
        after hours underground, how
                it meets the eye

straight on like a woman
      kneeling to gather
            what you needed

to give. My sister
      called herself Ruby,
            blurring the space around her

like a myth. Or maybe the myth
      is snow falling outside
            the club, her body

untouched by the precision
      of notes wincing
            in her hair, an alarm

in the dusk, how I still need
      to imagine her lit with silence
            before she rises

into another song, the color
      of light escaping a body, the blue-green eye
            at the center of a flame.

Last Night On Earth We Go To Wendy's

Starry-eyed and ravenous, we wait for it
to serenade us like a bullet singing to a wound. Is this
what you meant by romance? Me, scouring the remains
of my life over a pool of ketchup, thick as the spunk of creation
while the city blooms smoke, waiting to be swallowed?
Out of everything, I'll miss the oily contents of tin cans. Colored wrappers.
A fig eaten like a kiss in a stairwell. Your lips, potable wishes. The quiet
grace of Aphasia, the trans cashier who sells us fish sandwiches, her bright
wand of a smile and galactic tits orbiting the fryer. I want to make mind-
love, she says now to the darkness. All this glittering space
and no foreplay. Is this what you meant by loneliness? That stiff
feeling in my hips like rust and rain, a surgery that allows
the patient to watch. We are waiting for it
with graffitied hearts, to discolor and gouge the walls
of the restroom where stains blossom into gesture, fingerprints, a deliciousness
hard-earned and wreaking, brought down from the heavens
of grease, and I'm glad for once to have a body with fingernails and genitalia,
a tongue like a squatter's den that knows every violet edge of evening,
to unfold syllables from the book of silences, where we become
gentle, sipping endless refills, and saying thank you, even when it's obvious.

After Hours, Red Light District

She thumbed the spliff like a burning moth. A finger of light caught in a
      revolving door.
You need wings to get lifted. Our bodies half-lit against a revolving door.

I confettied the street outside the club, my legs writing bad checks on the pavement.
The bouncer's fist slashed a sunset, slapped me through the night's revolving door.

Puddle of milk. Split-open pod. The glass pipe navigated the armada blue
alleyway. We polished the moon's rib, held in the arms of a revolving door.

My fists unresolved in ash against her chest. All I ever wanted was a lap dance,
to sleep inside the half-built cathedral, absolved in the flesh's revolving doors,

to hear my name's dark end razored on her tongue. Spin me like a pigeon caught
in the airshaft, this heart of melted glass, flock of revolving doors.

The Vocalist

Commencement ceremony at the Tennessee Prison for Women

Next to the electric piano,
the prison's hush

a jukebox of confessions
and contraband-dazzlement,

the singer's tongue ignites
an invocation, music blurred

convex between her legs
the way I imagine

she taught herself
to feel good, syllables resuscitating

in her lungs, making each breath
poignant, a rawness

cutting through the gaze
of COs and visitors rising

for a better view. How undone, cold-
blooded would I be

to sing straight
for this crowd, notes released

my sister bent,
  pulling up her bunched panties
      asking me to look,
proud of the emblem
   cinched there

holding what will heal
  into another scar, this time entirely of her own

doing, and I still cannot witness
   where she bleeds into the gauze,
     where she will bleed, happily, for days.

Confession with Fire

*January 28, 1966: The Gilded Cage, a strip club in the Combat Zone of Boston,
burned to the ground in an electrical fire that consumed the entire block.*

I was looking to be trespassed,
    a shot glass of drizzle sucked
        from my navel,

to fall asleep on the steps of a church
    where dogs lick salt
        from the starfish

of my palms. I wanted the smell of leaves
    inked in her skin, maps
        of constellations,

the pulsing dark of starlings
    unraveling from a tree.
        Try catching the flare

of a note as it diminishes
    along the teeth of an upright,
        hands weaving ghosts

into air. I was looking for that
    kind of solitude, the hard love
        of snare throbbing

through her like a ravaged aura,
        fluorescent scent
                of aftermath, longing

soaked and illegible
        along the spine. Even God must love
                the color of a woman's dress

doused in applause, how you can feel
        every wrong note, bruised
                and shining to the core.

The Great American Challenge

You're out of place like an oyster
at a rodeo, the bartender's
        side-glance says, the honky-

tonk strip flushed with bullet-toed
        boots and beer signs,
                backwash of a juke-

box and someone's woman squiggling
        on the corner while "Freebird"
                gushes brand-new

from a convertible. I know a signifier
        when I see one: oysters in their ice
                beds at a catered dinner

party, imported from countries
        whose women smell like trade-
                offs and myth.

Who named the oyster
        aphrodisiac, superior
                to the ubiquitous clam?

Was it the sailor who invented
        mermaids after making love
                to manatees, taught

men to slit the mammal
        open when it clamped
                shut? I'm done with ambience.

I don't need to swallow
    a belly full of innuendo
        to feel desire—

I'm waiting for a real honest-
    to-god oyster made of flesh
        and humility,

to feel the hand's desperate tug
    reeling into cold
        and miraculous bloom

of low tide, and when the Great
    American Challenge
        rises like a missile in the back

of the sex store's throat, holy
    and oracular, taunting
        us to unhinge wide as we can,

I will hike up my inedible
    skirt like the crushed lip
        of an oyster,

climb the shiny peak
    of this immaculate stem,
        reciting every pledge

of allegiance I know, dripping
    wet for America, who keeps me
        safe from my own exploding heart.

After Hours, Nashville

Today the watercress spreading its itch
across a sewer pipe's runoff
cleaves to me like spoiled air.

Fluorescent speech malingers
the suburban landscape, shameless
and raw-mouthed

as a dress soaked in lover's sweat,
the flame of its tongue
and spiked consonants

blaring back vagrant pitch.
I've seen women hunched in the near-
dusk harvesting the bullet-tipped

leaves, trash bags bulging with carnage
like a sex shop where every vibrator
ignites at the slightest hint of heat,

a trillion prosthetic lips
mimicking human desire,
but watercress, I will not touch your

viper-booted limbs. I will not breathe
in the panic of your luster, douse
your shady lips with my toxic want.

You unzipper the darkness inside of me.
Your lounge singer's smile
smolders before rows of half-living stars.

If scarcity is the score we must live by, let me erupt
with you in the deadness of winter
dragging our peacocked tails

through unseasonal mud.
Let every inedible tendril be a pardon,
bloated with radiance.

Carnival, Provincetown

Like the aftermath of a riot,
　　　　streets ruptured
　　　　　　　and smoked

in disemboweled costumes,
　　　　spunk and latex
　　　　　　　glittering in the leaves,

Madonna's voice streams
　　　　through the parade,
　　　　　　　trucks strapped

with stereos and hard bodies,
　　　　so perfect it hurts
　　　　　　　to land the eye

on anything that doesn't shimmer,
　　　　tinseled intestines,
　　　　　　　immaculate against a glare.

Is it enough, now,
　　　　to pay attention when every
　　　　　　　voice and oiled

orifice refuses to be touched?
　　　　Madonna tells me
　　　　　　　to grab life by the cunt

but as a child I watched
　　　　men kiss in the streets, their leather
　　　　　　　chaps tight as tourniquets,

and prayed to be one
     of them, to love myself
          the way a match combusts

in a pocket. I want to take back
     the clear light of August
          humming at the end of the season,

wear it like a second sex,
     every blue-vesseled body
          and rippled gesture,

the under-glow of a world
     that no longer exists,
          to let what first

cut me open to the world
     be the only body I know:
          "Ray of Light" pouring through

me like a stranger's kiss,
     sifted in the chapel
          of vanishing arms.

God is a Capitalist

I, too, want honesty in exchange for my good money, a warm body
to accompany me when I'm lonely,

feeling the way trees must feel absorbing the used-up light
along highways, a song whose human-less pulse undoes me

as kindness undoes me, sometimes getting what I want
and wearing the smug look of a road gleaming from within,

how you know when someone, without meaning to, is telling you the truth—
my sister hustling, her lucite heels steeped in cash,

each of us loaded with expired magic. I'm talking about a weariness of stars, crooked
hope, the kind perfected in southern hemispheres where tourists go

buying up the spirit of revolution. We all want a lap dance
to mean something, and now, watching her up there

I can't say where she got it from, the drive to keep making something
beautiful out of it, glittering beyond recognition,

and it rips my goddamned heart out, watching it unfold as it must
every night, the story of our naked life.

Notes

The book's epigraph is from Terrance Hayes' poem "God is an American."

"Ode to the One-Liner" borrows a line from Marcus Wicker's poem "Maybe the Saddest Thing."

"The Barber Shop," "The Year I Worked in a Prison," "When it Rained," and "What I Loved" take place at the Suffolk County House of Corrections in Boston, Massachusetts. These poems are dedicated to the students and staff of the Offender Re-Entry Program.

"Vajazzled" refers to the trend of accessorizing/adorning one's vagina with gems.

The epigraph of "Through a Small Town" is from the *New York Times* article: "Hundreds Killed and Injured as Fuel Tanker Explodes in Congo." The poem is written after Ross Gay's poem "The Lion and the Gazelle."

"The Guitarist" is written after the photograph by William Claxton and is dedicated to my father.

"After Seeing The Misfits" refers to the film The Misfits (1961), directed by John Huston.

"Last Night On Earth We Go to Wendy's" is inspired by the form in which every end-word forms a complete line from another poem. The line is taken from Joe Wenderoth's *Letters to Wendy's*: "It is the creation of a quiet bright mind-space that allows for the deliciousness of genitalia to become obvious."

"The Vocalist": *COs* is the abbreviation for corrections officers.

"The Great American Challenge" refers to a type of dildo. The poem was written during the weeks leading up to the George Zimmerman trial.

"God is a Capitalist" is written after Terrance Hayes' poem "God is an American."